He Heru. A Comb

OBJECTS TALK BACK

About This Book Series
In collaboration with the Ethnologisches Museum and the Museum für Asiatische Kunst of the Staatliche Museen zu Berlin, the Stiftung Humboldt Forum im Berliner Schloss invited the writer Priya Basil to curate a series of events and books: *Objects Talk Back*.
Every year, Priya Basil asks two writers to engage with an object of their choice—either from the exhibited collection or from the museums' storage depots.
The project represents a new curatorial practice (complementing ongoing provenance research) characterized by transparency and dialogue regarding the collections in the Humboldt Forum, the complex history of its location and entanglements with contemporary global issues. The aim is to investigate the provenance history of the objects while simultaneously engaging in a direct dialogue with people biographically connected to the countries of origin, thereby fostering international multivocality and transforming museum practices.

Whiti Hereaka

He Heru. A Comb
An Ornament for the Most Sacred Part of the Body

HUMBOLDT FORUM

DIAPHANES

Heru
Ornamental comb made of whalebone
New Zealand, Aotearoa
19th century
27 x 7.5 x 1.5 cm
Inventory number: VI 408

The *heru* is a traditional Māori ornamental comb that reached Berlin in the nineteenth century. Such combs were not used for hair care but served as a sign of high rank. The object entered the collections of the Berlin Völkerkundemuseum (today the Ethnologisches Museum, Staatliche Museen zu Berlin) via the Royal Prussian Art Collection. The circumstances under which the object was acquired in New Zealand are not documented.

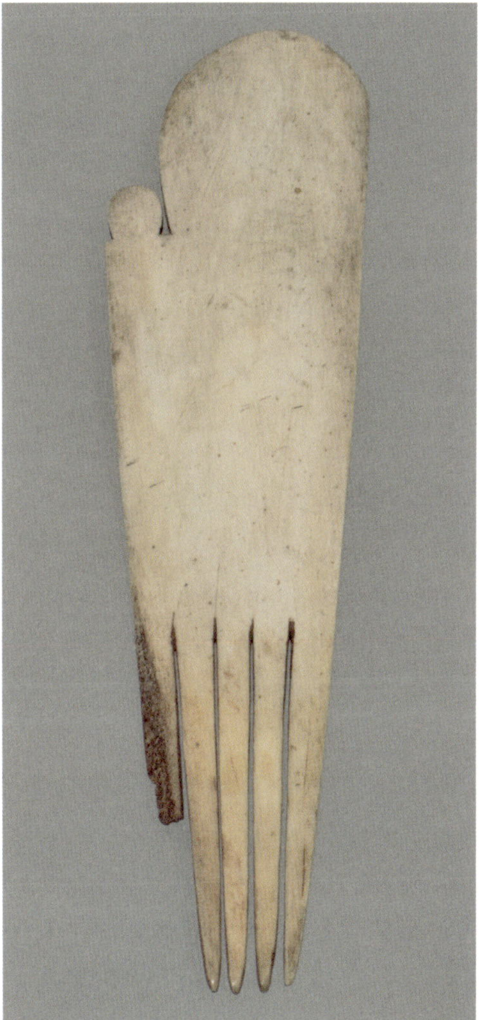

OBJECTS TALK BACK

Objects have voices, which we may not hear. Literature helps us to listen.

Objects Talk Back is a project that asks: what are the possibilities of literature to open up new stories, questions and relations when writers engage with museum archives?

While there are promising currents of change, ethnological museum collections remain tied to violent colonial histories and ongoing practices of domination. Information for most objects is still limited to date of creation or acquisition, place of origin, type of material, collector or donator. Even these details are not always accurate.

The archaeologist Dan Hicks proposes "necrography," a practice of digging into the past to trace the colonial story behind an object.[1] Such an approach may reveal much of value, but also leave one "straining against the limits of the archive," as literary scholar Saidiya Hartman writes.[2]

Colonial archives contain their own prejudices and distortions. Hartman suggests "critical fabulation"—melding history, theory and fiction—"to displace the received or authorized account." Inspired by these ideas, I coined the term "fabulography" for *Objects Talk Back*. In a piece for *British Art Studies*, I describe fabulography as an invitation to work creatively with-from-through gaps, facts and imagination to expand the narrative space around an object.[3] Fabulography involves digging deep, uncovering painful details, but also rising up, celebrating, honoring, reconnecting.

Since 2021, two writers are invited each year to explore collections of the Ethnologisches Museum and the Museum für Asiatische Kunst, both part of the Staatliche Museen zu Berlin. The writers encounter objects displayed in the Humboldt Forum, Berlin, and also those stored in the museums' depots. They select an object, and respond however they wish—through fiction, poetry, narrative nonfiction, multimedia texts. Later, they present the finished work at a live event in the Humboldt

Forum. Now, objects talk back in a book series as well, affirming Hartman's appeal "to consider stories as a form of compensation, perhaps the only kind we will ever receive."[4]

Priya Basil

1 Dan Hicks, "Necrography: Death-Writing in the Colonial Museum," *British Art Studies*, Issue 19, 2021: https://doi.org/10.17658/issn.2058-5462/issue-19/conversation. | **2** Saidiya Hartman, "Venus in Two Acts," *Small Axe* (Indiana University) 12, no. 2 (2008): https://muse.jhu.edu/search?action=browse&limit=publisher_id:3 (accessed March 9, 2024). | **3** Priya Basil, "Writing to Life," *British Art Studies*, Issue 19, 2021: https://www.britishartstudies.ac.uk/issues/issue-index/issue-19/death-writing-in-the-colonial-museums (accessed March 9, 2024). | **4** Hartman, "Venus in Two Acts."

Priya Basil

Introduction

Stories, stories, stories—our lives are colored and shaped by them: when we gather and share gossip, or sit silently alone with a book—the words come alive in our minds... The stories live through us and us through them.[1]

Whiti Hereaka

Do we make stories, or do stories make us? This eternal dialectic sits at the heart of Whiti Hereaka's oeuvre. She explores it in many ways, most excitingly through form. Structure itself, she shows, shapes story. Every work she creates has an entirely new, unique structure. In the book *You Are Here*, a collaboration with artist Peata Larkin, Whiti's text is "based on the Fibonacci sequence starting at three: the words spiral out to the center of the book and then spiral back."[2] Larkin observed that the form of the text "describes so eloquently the struggle of finding our way back home to our Māori roots."[3]

What would emerge from the object—a *heru*, a comb—that Whiti decided to engage with at the Humboldt Forum? A heru: "an ornament for the most sacred part of the body." An ornament with five teeth, one of them broken.

Whiti Hereaka is a novelist and playwright of Māori and Pākehā descent. Her *iwi*, or kinship group, affiliations are Ngāti Tūwharetoa, Te Arawa, Ngāti Whakaue, Tūhourangi, Ngāti Tumatawera, Tainui. She lives in Wellington, on the north island of Aotearoa / New Zealand. She teaches creative writing at Massey University and is a board member of the Māori Literature Trust where one of the programs, Te Papa Tupu,[4] is aimed at supporting emerging Māori writers working in all genres.

Several of Whiti's plays have been produced and won awards. She admits to a special affection for the term "playwright" because it "implies that words must be worked and wrought." A "wright" means someone who makes or builds things, especially out of wood. "I am pushing to be a 'wrighter' instead of a 'writer,'" Whiti has said.[5]

Her novels include *The Graphologist's Apprentice*, *Bugs*, *Legacy* and *Kurangaituku*. In 2019, her novel *Legacy* won a New Zealand Book Award for Children and Young Adults. *Kurangaituku* was awarded the 2022 Jann Medlicott Acorn Award for Fiction, a prize of the Ockham New Zealand Book Awards, and was long listed for the Dublin Literary Award in 2023. Kurangaituku, the bird-woman of the book's title, will again make an appearance in a new novel, *Ariā*, as will an object from a German museum—the Rauru Māori *wharenui*, or meeting house, which is at the MARKK ethnology museum in Hamburg.

Kurangaituku is a retelling of the myth of Hatupatu, a Māori boy, encountering the apparently monstrous, nameless bird-woman. The novel has three parts. To read each of the two longer parts, the book literally has to be turned over and started from the other end. This physical act, Whiti has said, mirrors the main character's world turning upside down, as well as a movement between the Underworld and the earthly realm above. With this form, Whiti also evades linearity, unfurling a narrative that swirls time and space, spinning its characters and readers in unending loops with different beginnings and endings. *Do we make stories, or do stories make us?*

In *He Heru*, her *Objects Talk Back* text, Whiti confesses that her first impression of the object she chose was "underwhelming": "This heru seems not only unadorned, but unfinished. A blank waiting to be honed." That very quality becomes an invitation. Into the blankness Whiti brings "embellishment," elaborately adorning the heru with stories. From a seemingly simple whalebone comb, she creates an intricate mirror work of reverence and beauty. A text in nine sections, "a part for each tooth, and a part for each space between them." The parts tell of love, loss, longing. They include stories of whales from whose bones the objects were made, of Māori gods and the power of women, of colonial whalers fishing their prey almost to extinction in the South Pacific, of a carver creating a comb, of a writer who cuts her hair and moves across worlds weaving connections.

Kurangaituku's narrative encompasses the earth's ancient geologic cycles of extinction and creation, the evolution of multiple life forms, the perspective of more-than-human beings who inhabited the island before the Māori, or Song Makers, came and long before the arrival of colonizers, or "new people." The bird-woman, hungry for life after a cataclysmic event, gorges herself on the stories of the Song Makers: "I fed on their idea of me, allowing it to divide my cells and rebuild my body."[6] She is recreated in the act, but it is a violent process: "their storytelling tore my body apart."[7] Stories can hurt, even when we choose them. But the ones we do not, or cannot, choose are often the most destructive. At one point in the novel, Hinenuitepō, goddess of the night and the dead, reflects:

> *New people and new ways have come, spreading out over the land. Bringing new ways to die. Bringing new stories and their own gods... The newcomers hoard land and resources... They kill birds not to eat, but to collect the bodies and display them. They collect many things for display, these new ones—insects, leaves, images and stories. They collect my children's stories to preserve them, but corrupt the telling with their own narratives. This is how I became a monster, through their telling.*[8]

This is also how Kurangaituku became a "monster, ogress, thing." Whiti's novel, narrated from the bird-woman's perspective, restores agency, beauty and power to the mythical figure. Whiti has said, "the only place where the women's voices in pūrākau, myths, have been silenced are in the retellings that originated with British ethnologists that published our stories and put their own patriarchal lens on them. It is unfortunate that *those* retellings of our stories have become the ones that we are most familiar with."[9] *Do we make stories, or do stories make us?*

Through her writing, Whiti has been decolonizing Māori creation stories and reshaping Western literary forms, such as the novel, to a more Māori way of storytelling. She points out that "Pūrākau may be fabulous and fantastic but they are also real... Nor is there any separation of the 'fanciful' stories of our origin, i.e. mythology and folklore, from the believable or factual, the real from the imagined, rational from the irrational, or what can be believed in and what cannot. Māori do not make those distinctions. It is all history, fluid, holistic, inclusive—not necessarily linear—and it may be being told backwards, which is why, to orient ourselves, we always place our origin stories in front. The stories are actually the beginning of a whakapapa, a genealogy. And what they establish is the beginning of a distinctive world view."[10] It is such a world view that Whiti opens up around *He Heru.*

On each visit to Berlin, Whiti came bearing small, thoughtful gifts for the *Objects Talk Back* team, all of whom were strangers the first time. She brought the same generosity to the collections. Accompanied by curator Dorothea Deterts, she approached the objects from Aotearoa with openness, curiosity, delight. It was a joyful experience to encounter this heritage in Whiti's presence. Even being in the storage depot was less dreadful with her. All who go there are obliged to wear safety gear against traces of highly toxic, potentially cancer-causing pesticides, including DDT, with which objects made from wood, leather, or feathers were historically sprayed to prevent infestation and damage by insects. Indiscriminate spraying and the proximity of stored objects meant that those items not treated with the chemicals were also contaminated. Whiti signed the consent form confirming she was aware of the risks, donned a white coat, FFP2 mask, and blue latex gloves, then added her own extra layer of protection. She recited *karakia,* Māori prayers, before entering the dim, cool, light- and temperature-controlled rooms. "I wish I had something like that," I said. I had been in the storage rooms for East African cultural heritage for the first time earlier that day, with the writer Maaza Mengiste who was also researching for *Objects Talk Back*, and the shadow of the visit still lay thickly upon me. "Don't worry. I've said *karakia* for us all," Whiti replied.

After we emerged from the storage, she flicked some drops of water over herself, for *whakanoa*. She explained that this Māori practice helped smooth the shift between different energy states or spaces. *Noa*, she said, signifies being "ordinary or normal," and is paired with *whaka*, a prefix to turn nouns into verbs—hence, whakanoa, the act of becoming ordinary or normal. "Grounding" might be a good English equivalent. She encouraged me to try the ritual. It definitely helped. Yet, no doubt, the lighter mood was also influenced by Whiti's observations on the nature of the Māori objects in the Berlin collections. From what she could see, most of these objects were created for the European market or could plausibly have been given away by the Māori. Beautiful as they were, many of the objects were likely not the most precious and sacred pieces of Māori heritage. "I don't sense here the kind of violence associated with collections from other places"—which is not to minimize the brutal violence that defined colonialism in Aotearoa.

Manaakitanga is a core Māori value and practice. The term is commonly translated as "hospitality" in English. Professor Te Kani Kingi, a Māori scholar, defines the term as "behavior featuring generosity, care, respect and reciprocity towards others."[11] Whiti Hereaka embodies manaakitanga; all she is, all she creates, flows from, through, back to it—within a wider web of responsibility, accountability, relationality. Thus, Whiti makes clear at the very start of *He Heru*: "Understand that in accepting this taonga that we are establishing a relationship—you cannot just take, you must give in return." The text goes on to show colonialism as the antithesis of manaakitanga, an insatiable taking that destroys all it touches, depleting the vitality of humans, whales, waters, life.

When she departed after her research visit, Whiti did not immediately say which object she had chosen, but hinted her response would extend beyond text: "I think I'll need to sew something, plus maybe ... we'll see," she

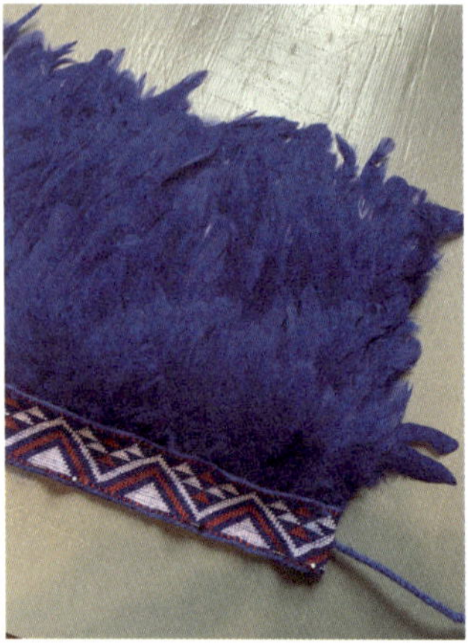

Kākahu Māori, a feather cloak made by Whiti Hereaka

said, hands flying, as if already warming up. She began work on a text made from strands of fiction and memoir, myth and history, and simultaneously on a *tāniko*, a handwoven band of red, blue and white, which she patterned to look like shark teeth, and to which she later attached rows of electric-blue feathers. (She would wear it, like a sash, over the blue outfit she stitched for her *Objects Talk Back* performance, along with mako shark teeth earrings—the embellishments adding bite to the invocation of her text: "Let my words have teeth.")

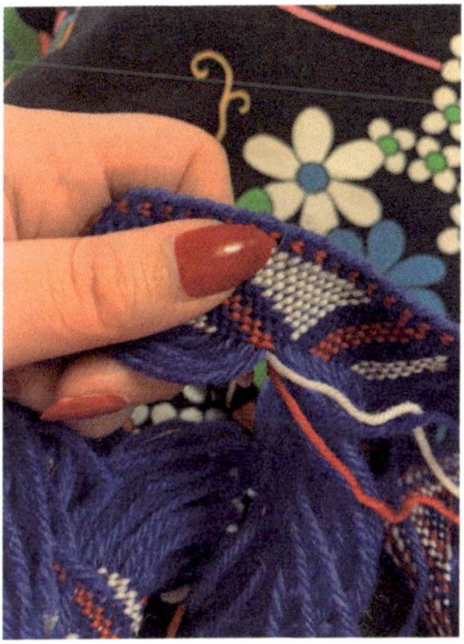

Woven trim for the Kākahu Māori

Whiti also began laying down dozens of layers of paint on board, a technique used to make an acrylic surface thick enough to carve into. She knew this project would not be ready in time for the event, but that was not the point; it was the process that mattered: "in the planning and thinking and layering of [the paint], I found a way into the writing." To complete her tribute, Whiti the wrighter carved a replica of the heru from wood. (She would wear it at her *Objects Talk Back* event, pulling it from her hair while reading aloud her version of a myth about Taranga, a powerful female figure in the Māori cosmology.)

"Let us first build a whare where we can share our stories. A whare tapere: a house of storytelling and games. A pātaka kōrero: a storehouse of language."[12] So Whiti wrote in the prologue to *Pūrākau: Māori Myths Retold by Māori Writers*. She began her event at the Humboldt Forum in a similar vein. The foyer of the reconstructed palace building, where most *Objects Talk Back* events happen, is a huge atrium, with the roof looming fifty meters above a pale natural stone floor. The vastness and coldness are somewhat mitigated within the circle of the Mechanical Arena, a mobile stage constructed like a mini amphitheater. It is always incredible to witness *Objects Talk Back* authors and stories inhabit this space within the space, making it at once bigger and smaller and warmer. Whiti inaugurated the evening with *karakia*:

Tuia ki runga
Tuia ki raro
Tuia ki roto
Tuia ki waho
Tuia te here tangata
Tūturu o whiti

Whakamaua, ki tīna!

Tīna!

Haumi e, hui e

Taiki e!

Stitch the celestial energies

To the terrestrial energies

Within

And without

Bind the kinship strands of humanity

Permanent, consistent are the fibers of light

Draw these matters to a single point and give them substance

The wisdom is bound, it collects

It is held![13]

Whiti then situated herself in a genealogy that includes human as well as more-than-human ancestors. Next, placing herself in Berlin, she acknowledged the waters of the nearby River Spree. Her words wove a shelter that enveloped the arena. She invited the audience to join the incantation by repeating certain phrases. In the course of this

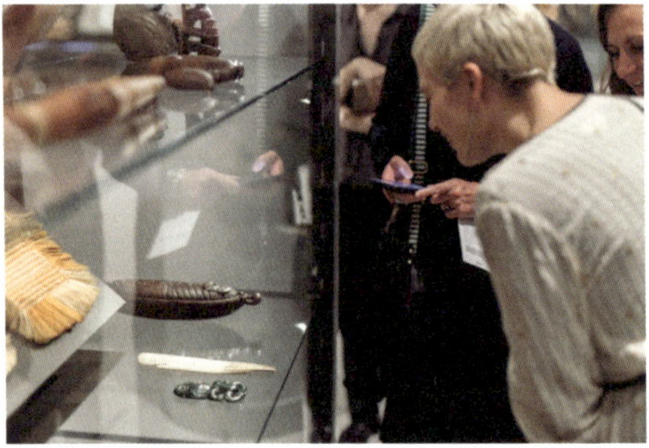

He Heru. A Comb. View of the exhibition during the event with Whiti Hereaka at the Humboldt Forum, 2024

call and response, individuals chorused into community. We were in Whiti's whare. And the storytelling began.

She unfurls a stunning cosmology around the heru, combing with it through time and space to make "stories of ocean blue, blood red, bone white," thus shattering the silence left by the museum description *Zugang ungeklärt*, "source unknown." The museum's "*heru* that has never been worn" becomes "a *heru* that will be worn and loved" through Whiti's writing, sewing, painting, carving. "And with each generation that wears it, its voice will deepen with resonance."

As the *Objects Talk Back* project continues and develops through the participation of different writers like Whiti, the bounds of literature are expanded. Inspired by the objects—whose stories come as song, rhythm, color, ritual, scent—writers become wrighters, building with more than words. In this way, they honor ancient and indigenous ways of knowing, multisensory, multiform.

Do we make stories, or do stories make us?

1 Whiti Hereaka and Witi Ihimaera, eds., *Pūrākau: Māori Myths Retold by Māori Writers* (Auckland: Penguin Books New Zealand, 2019). | **2** Whiti Hereaka and Peata Larkin, *You Are Here* (Auckland: Massey University Press, 2025), p. 94. | **3** Ibid. | **4** I asked Whiti what the name means and she said, "It can be translated literally as 'incubator' (or perhaps a container of growth—but the way the container is named suggests something treasured within)." | **5** Thom Conroy, "Writing First for Māori Readers: An Interview with Whiti Hereaka," *Headland* 18, n.d., https://headland.org.nz/issues/issue-18/interview-with-whiti-hereaka/ (accessed December 22, 2025). | **6** Whiti Hereaka, *Kurangaituku* (Wellington: Huia Publishers, 2021), p. 35. | **7** Ibid., p. 37. | **8** Ibid., p. 101. | **9** Stella Chrysostomou, "Story Sovereignty: An Interview with Whiti Hereaka," *Volume* (May 9, 2022), https://volume.nz/volumebooks/2022/05/fighting-against-structure-interview.html. | **10** Elizabeth Heritage, "How Language and Storytelling Shape Reality in *Kurangaituku* by Whiti Hereaka," *Reactor* (February 1, 2022), https://reactormag.com/how-language-and-storytelling-shape-reality-in-kurangaituku-by-whiti-hereaka/. | **11** Te Kani Kingi et al., *Te Puawaitanga O Ngā Whānau: Six Markers of Flourishing Whānau. A Discussion Document* (Palmerston North: Massey University, 2014), p. 14, https://knowledgeauckland.org.nz/media/1403/six-markers-of-flourishing-whanau-2014_kingi-t.pdf. | **12** Hereaka and Ihimaera, *Pūrākau.* | **13** "Karakia: Incantation," Massey University, https://www.massey.ac.nz/student-life/m%C4%81ori-at-massey/te-reo-m%C4%81ori-and-tikanga-resources/te-reo-m%C4%81ori-pronunciation-and-translations/karakia-incantation/(accessed December 22, 2025).

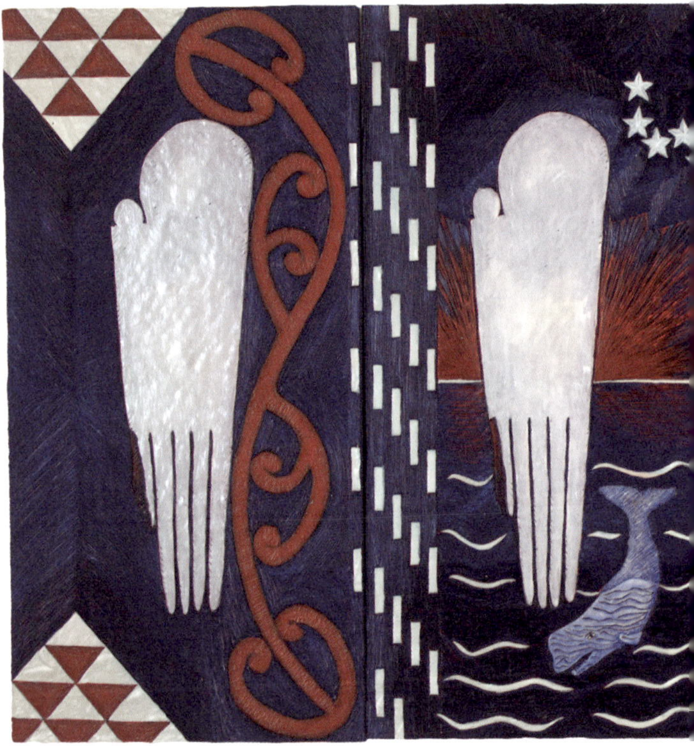

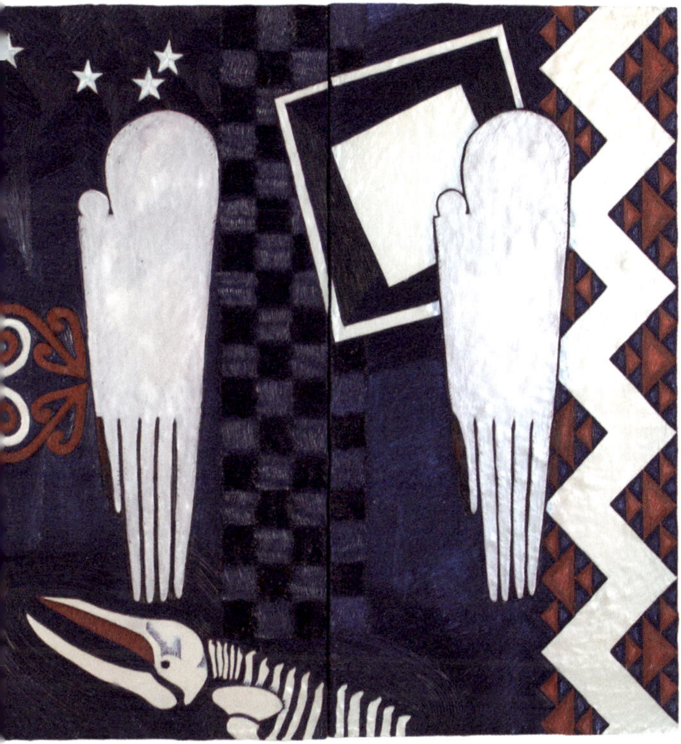

Whiti Hereaka, He Heru, 2025

Whiti Hereaka

He Heru. A Comb
An Ornament for the Most Sacred Part of the Body

tahi

If there is one thing you should know about me, it is that I'm not shy of embellishment. In every sense of the word, really.

There is truth to what I say, although not always fidelity. Trust me when I tell you that I'm reliably unreliable. Although, painfully authentic—I tend to wear my *art* on my sleeve.

I come from Te Arawa, an *iwi* famed for our performances for *tauiwi*. European tourists would—and still do—visit our *rohe* to take the healing waters and to witness the wonders of our geyser land. The world came to us and of course we went to the world as well.

It was de rigueur in the nineteenth century to have a living exhibit—a native to give context to the goods on display. We were a curiosity then—and now—whale bone in our hair and in the English corsets that constricted our *hope.*

We sang songs to people ignorant of their meaning, locked away in a language they didn't understand.

We were misread—our *taonga* of objects and language seen as mere ornamentation. Instead, each supports the story of us, carries our voices. Without understanding meaning, we become merely shapes and sounds. Blanks for other stories to be projected onto, nonsense poems for lazy avant-gardists.[1]

I am not that far removed from my people who came to Europe to tell our stories, sing our songs, give voice to our culture—five generations at the most. Almost two hundred years between us, and yet here I am, as I live and breathe, making an exhibition of myself.

Now that I have your attention, let my words have teeth.

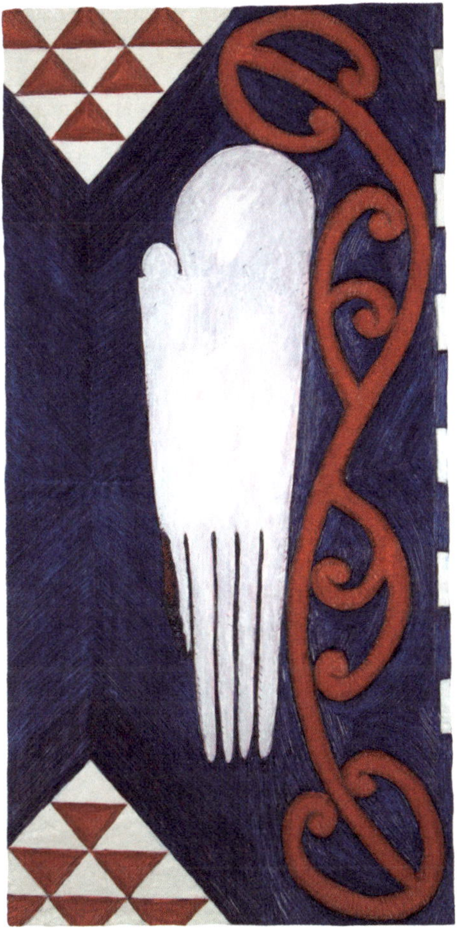

Whiti Hereaka, He Heru, panel 1: Tahi—Niho taniwha (Teeth of Taniwha) / Shape—Mangōpare (Hammerhead shark) / Rua—Roimata (Teardrops)

I will tell you stories of ocean blue, blood red, bone white.

Understand that in accepting this taonga, we are establishing a relationship—you cannot just take, you must give in return.

Heru—comb.

Tahi—one.

Te Arawa—a tribal group from the central North Island.

Iwi—tribal group.

Tauiwi—strangers, foreigners.

Rohe—area of land, territory.

Hope—waist; here I am playing with "hope" in English too.

Taonga—treasure, precious thing.

shape

The carver holds the bone in his hand, feeling the weight of it—the creature it once was and the object it will become.

Tohorā are a gift from Tangaroa. When one is found on the beach, no part is wasted. The people collect the bones and teeth and bring them to the carver. Sometimes he will carve the bones fresh. Sometimes he'll wait a season or two for it to dry and deepen the grain.

He looks at the bone, turning it to find where he will cut. His idea is half-formed.

A heru, an ornament for the most sacred part of the body.

He squints his eyes to pull a pattern from the grain of the bone, to see the story it will tell of its maker and of its wearer.

He still doesn't know who will wear it.

He roughs out the shape, a blank waiting for him to hone it.

The carver leaves plenty of space above the teeth of the comb to shape its story—the large curve at the top could hold *mangōpare*, suggesting that the person who wears this heru leads with the same strength, courage and tenacity of the hammerhead shark.

He thinks of the shark's teeth she wears on her earlobes—the base of the teeth painted blood red. She is known to be incisive, her remarks biting. Some men, slow-witted and tongue-tied, find these traits to be unattractive. Such men leave her …

Unimpressed.

He must admit, though, that his own words have dried in his mouth when she smiled at him, under the flash of her eyes.

Why can he not be as eloquent with his speech as he is with his chisel?

This heru, then, will be hers. And he will carve everything he wants to tell her: the mangōpare for the strength he admires in her, *pūhoro* to speak of his own agility.

Or perhaps a *manaia*—so she is protected from any ill will against her.

Or perhaps a *koru*—for the new life he hopes to make with her, his seed uncurling in her womb.

And there are so many ideas, so many things that he wants to say to her that he cannot do anything at all.

The carver holds the bone in his hand, feeling the weight of it.

Tohorā—general term for "whale," although in particular for baleen whales. Here, I am using it generally.
Tangaroa—deity of the sea.
Mangōpare—a motif in Māori art.
Pūhoro—a motif in Māori art.
Manaia—a motif in Māori art.
Koru—a motif in Māori art.

rua

Of hair and bone. Two women who lent their power to a demigod.

When I was a child, I read and reread the picture books of these stories. But in those, these women were called Māui's mother and Māui's grandmother. I learnt their names much, much later.

Taranga pulls the heru from her hair with such force that one of its teeth cracks and breaks off. She lets the comb fall to the sand. She walks closer to the waves, letting the wind loosen her hair. She doesn't care if it tangles and knots, she will sacrifice it to her grief anyway.

She has given birth to her youngest child, her *pōtiki*, Māui. He left her womb too soon—he is not fully formed.

His small, lifeless body is now curled on the beach, still attached to his *whenua*.

She wades in the water, letting the sea wash away the blood on her thighs. The salt she tastes could be her tears, her *hupe*, the spray from the sea. It doesn't matter—her pain is so overwhelming that it spills out into the world around her.

Ocean, tears, blood, mucus.

The cries of the *karoro*, circling above her, could be her own.

Enough. She will dwell in her mourning later, now she must tend to her boy.

Taranga cuts her long, thick hair and wraps Māui, her beloved *pēpi*, in it. Nestled in this new womb of warm, black waves, Māui is gifted to the sea.

Thus, when Māui reaches the shore of his grandfather, he is born a second time.

Murirangawhenua pulls her jawbone free from her head with such care that the teeth are left—although worn down from years of eating *aruhe*—firm in their sockets.

She hands her jaw to her *mokopuna*, her grandson Māui. Although he is still a young man, she knows that he will do great, miraculous things. Particularly now that he holds her *mātauranga* in his hands—the bone is dense with power, years of *kupu* and *karakia* thrumming through it.

Blood, bone, words, power.

Before she muted herself, she had taught him the stories and the words he needs to know to tame the sun and to land a fish so big that his people will live upon it.

But he is a young man, rash and impulsive, so she worries that he will forget her voice, focusing instead on fashioning *patu* and *matau*, club and hook, from her jaw.

She would remind him again of where the *real* power lies, but without her jaw she cannot form the words. She is powerless.

The jawbone nestled in his hands, Māui has already turned away from her. And so, this story turns away from her too.

Rua—two.

Māui—the trickster demigod common throughout Polynesia.

Taranga—mother of Māui.

Pōtiki—youngest child.

Whenua—in this instance: placenta; but it also means "land," so I'm playing with both meanings.

Hupe—nasal mucus.

Karoro—kelp gull, Dominican gull (*Larus dominicanus*).

Pēpi—baby.

Murirangawhenua—grandmother of Māui.

Aruhe—fernroot, a staple of the Māori diet pre-contact; it is very fibrous and would wear the molar teeth smooth.

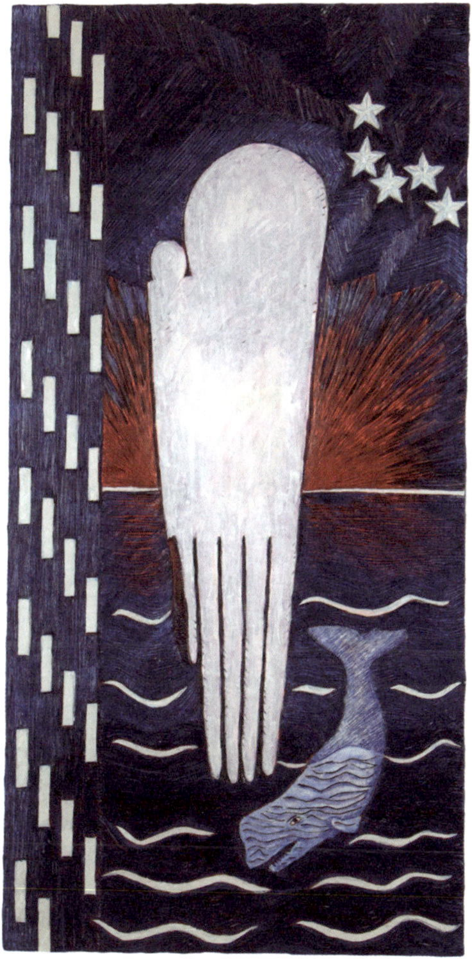

Whiti Hereaka, He Heru, panel 2: Rua—Roimata (Teardrops), Ocean—Scrimshaw whale, Toru—The constellation Matariki (The Pleiades)

Mokopuna—descendant, grandchild.

Mātauranga—knowledge, wisdom, education.

Kupu—word(s).

Karakia—incantation, prayer.

ocean

The whaler is carving scrimshaw on a sperm whale's tooth. He uses what he has to hand—the worthless teeth of the beast, his knife and some lamp-black to carve a keepsake to take home. It is a sort of prayer, then, the hope that he will make it home from the vast wildness of the South Pacific.

The pursuit of whales has taken ships further and further south. These men are not on a foolish hunt for the great antipodean continent, but rather to satisfy more prosaic needs: this sperm whale will yield oil that burns bright and clean, oil that lubricates the machines in factories. If they catch a Southern Right, then its blubber will be rendered, and its baleen dried to make the bones in corsets.

Perhaps later tonight he will allow himself to think of loosening the lacing on her corset, of her body beneath her fine linen chemise, of the weight of her against him.

For now, and until the call goes up that a spout or fluke has been spotted, he will concentrate on the scene he is creating. In the center of the tooth, he carves a likeness of its former body—a sperm whale in its entirety. There is something akin to glee in its eye and he can't bear the thought of making it invisible beneath the waves, so instead of crosshatching it like its tail, he carves delicate waves over its head and body as if it is about to breach.

Life at sea is merciless and often boring. He hopes that they might put ashore soon at Kororāreka, so he can be among the company of other ships—whalers or sealers, he doesn't care as long as he doesn't have to hear the same stories from the mates onboard this ship once again.

The town is rough, mainly because of men like him, but the land is beautiful. Perhaps he should take leave of the sea, travel inland and go native. Take a wife—the women are comely enough—and become a *Pākehā* Māori, learn their undulating tongue and wear their tattoo on his face.

In that country, men like him can marry princesses and own good, fertile land. He could be an interpreter—striking deals between the tribe and the land agents or selling bits of native tat to the European collectors for their exhibitions and curiosity cabinets.

He would be a curiosity himself—a civilized man turned savage.

The dream will fade with the afternoon sun. Ah, the lives he has lived while the whales elude them—the places he has lived in his mind almost as plentiful as the women he's thought of bedding. Another day without a catch.

And another.

And another.

Kororāreka—also known as Russell, a town in the Bay of Islands (North Island), the first significant European settlement and seaport in New Zealand; before the Treaty of Waitangi, the town had a reputation of being lawless and of the European inhabitants acting badly.

Pākehā—white New Zealanders (mainly of British descent).

Māori—the general term for the indigenous peoples of New Zealand.

toru

Three stories about whales.

Wellington harbor was once a breeding ground for Southern Right Whales, or tohorā, before they were hunted to near extinction. They would travel northward from Antarctica, in the cold winter months of July and August, before migrating southward in spring. There were so many that a visitor to Wellington in the late 1800s complained that their songs kept him up all night.

To stave off insomnia, at night I stream whale song on my iPhone.

In 1912, the bones of an entire pod of sperm whales were found at the top of a cliff on Miramar Peninsula. The bones were so old that they crumbled when they were touched, and they were unmarked by tools used by Māori pre-contact. How the bones ended up at the top of a cliff, forty-five meters above sea level, was a bit of a mystery. Successive earthquakes had only risen the peninsula around nine meters in the past twenty thousand years or so. The theory was that they were washed there by a great tsunami.

I live on the isthmus between Wellington harbor and Miramar Peninsula and know that the tsunami safe-zone lines painted on the hill behind me are much, much lower than thirty meters.

Lately, whales have been returning to the harbor. It has taken decades, but the laws, sanctuaries, and conservation efforts have made this a literal safe harbor. There are always pods of dolphins, and occasionally orcas chasing stingray close to the city—but the tohorā are coming back too. In 2018, the mayor called off a fireworks display in the harbor because a Southern Right Whale had been visiting for over a week. We called the whale Matariki for the holiday the fireworks were to celebrate. There was another whale visit in 2023—not Matariki this time, but

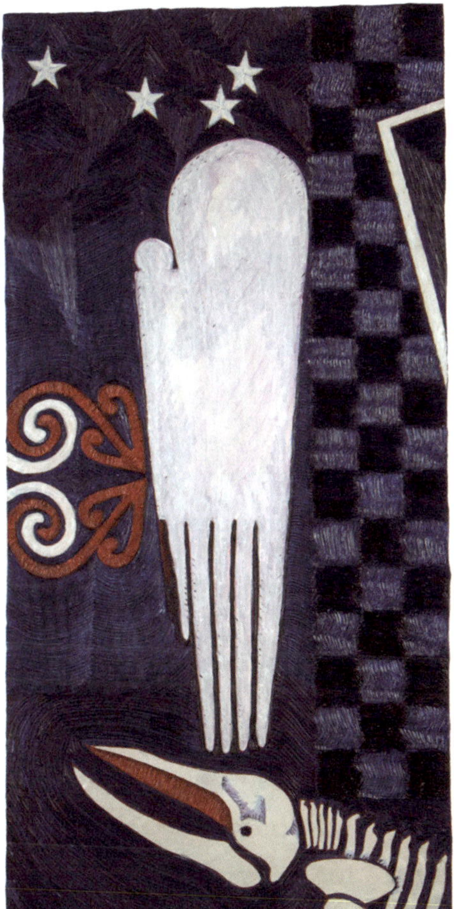

Whiti Hereaka, He Heru, panel 3: Toru—The constellation Matariki and ngaru (Ocean wave, here a tsunami) / Bone—Blue Whale Skeleton / Whā—waves of paint

another young whale. They say this could indicate a growth in population of up to seven percent.

I learnt that *bālaena* is Latin for "whale." I have walked along Balaena Bay many times, ignorant of the history of it locked away in a language that I don't know. The water is quiet.

Toru—three.
Matariki—refers to the rising of the Pleiades, celebrated as Māori New Year.

bone

The artist has seldom had the chance to work with *parāoa* before. He feels the weight of it—through the taonga, he will create the voice of the tohorā, which will be carried for many generations. He looks for the shape of that voice in the bone that he holds.

The tohorā was stranded on a beach in the rohe of the artist's iwi. These days, if efforts to refloat whales are unsuccessful, there are government departments to contact and permits to file before the whale can be harvested. More importantly, there are *atua* to thank, *tikanga* to observe, and the whale—*tuākana* to humanity—is given a name. This whale was a *kuia*, and so, in the *mihi* to her, her long life was acknowledged.

The Crown hadn't let iwi harvest from whales right up until the artist was a kid. It irks him a bit—all the treaties and regulations are a response to pākehā exploitation of *te taiao*, yet it's Māori who have a finger wagged at them when they practice their customs. Pākehā create a problem, and Māori have to bear those consequences.

The knowledge of how to harvest from the whale had been severed from his iwi years ago. They had to call in *tohunga* from other rohe to teach them.

She was a blue whale, so the bones, sinew, and baleen were harvested. The rest of the body was buried in the sand. Diggers chugged along the tideline—their bright orange a shock against the blue of the sky, the white of the sand, the red of the blood.

He looks at the bone, imagining where he will make his first cut. This material is so precious that he must be careful with his cuts—precise, efficient, and economical.

Still, the parāoa inspires him to push his *mahi toi* further. It calls to be crafted into something that pushes the limits of his skill. And yet, perhaps it is a true measure of mastery to embrace simplicity—to let the parāoa, to let the tohorā, speak for itself.

It wants to sing of beauty and *mana*. It will lend its voice to the story of the artist and the wearer.

He cuts a long, slender slab. Roughs out the shape, seeing the object it will become. He incises between the five teeth of the heru.

A heru that will be worn and loved. And with each generation that wears it, its voice will deepen with resonance.

Parāoa—whale bone.

Atua—deities.

Tikanga—rules, the right way of doing things.

Tuākana—elder sibling (usually of the same sex). Humanity was created by Tānemahuta after all other living creatures (including trees and plants) were made;

therefore, as our elders, they deserve our respect.

Kuia—elderly woman, grandmother; a term of respect.

Mihi—acknowledgement or thanks. Here, a speech of acknowledgement of the whale's life and her connection to the place and people.

Te taiao—the natural world, environment.

Tohunga—expert.

Mahi toi—art, craft.

Mana—prestige, power. We all have inherent mana, but it can also be enhanced or lost by the way we live our lives and the values we uphold in our community.

whā

I'm layering paint onto four boards. I pull the paint-laden brush down the panels in undulating waves of ultramarine. In the next layer, the waves will be horizontal. The brush I chose—for house painting rather than anything fine—is coarse enough to leave ridges in the paint so when the light catches, it looks like hair, or etched waves in a printed sea. I'm building up layers so that eventually the boards will be so thick with paint that I can carve into them.

It has taken over a week to get to almost twenty layers, and I'm aiming for at least fifty because I have a tendency to dig deep. I'm probably delusional to think that I can finish these pieces to accompany my writing—the preparation of the boards themselves will take weeks to complete; it takes longer for the paint to dry in the cold wet of winter. But in the planning and thinking and layering of them, I found a way into the writing.

Back in 2020, I went to a workshop to learn this technique from an artist who has been paint-carving for years. In the summer she would layer the students' boards in alabaster white—at least thirty layers before we added the final three coats of color in the winter. Among the birds and flowers carved in that workshop, I chose instead an anatomical human heart, the bright white of my lines veining through the top coats of blood red.

I went to the workshop as research for my next novel—a way to get to know my protagonist, an artist, or probably more accurately, a way to get to know her practice. It was the kind of busywork I chide my

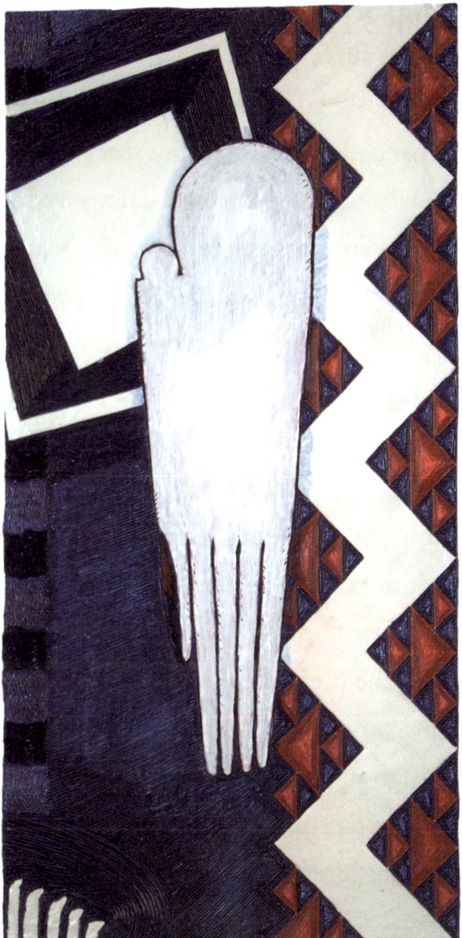

Whiti Hereaka, He Heru, panel 4: Whā—waves of paint / Object—
Humboldt Forum Logo / Rima—Aramoana (Pathway to the sea)

students for. A kind of wittering while they wait for inspiration to surface.

I didn't *need* to go to the workshop, I already knew all that I needed to flesh out my story: the layers of paint like *whakapapa*—both genealogy and geology, of generations and of sedimentation.

My character would carve, and it would be an act of subversion, perhaps even transgression—claiming a space that is almost always thought of as male.

But there was also something in the action of it—of revealing things hidden deep below the surface.

I didn't *need* to go to the workshop, but there *is* something about holding the tool in your own hand, in knowing the pressure of blade against surface, in how your carving can change as the paint warms and cools throughout the day.

There is something in physically being there, in creating something instead of just imagining it.

Whā—four.

Whakapapa—genealogy, which to Māori includes

mountains, bodies of water, the canoe their ancestors arrived in, the place their tribe originates from, the area of their sub-tribe, their ancestors, their family. At the very end of this genealogy is their own name. *Whakapapa* also literally means "to layer ground," so I'm playing with both meanings.

object

The writer first sees the heru online.

She had awoken to an email inviting her to give voice to an object that had lost its own long ago. The institution was on the other side of the world, so of course it must be a scam—why would they invite *her* to visit? She turned the idea of it over in her head, tried to get the measure of it. If it *was* a scam, why would they target her? As a writer, she has so little of anything of worth at all.

A handful of stories, a knack for twisting words into pleasing shapes. She can carve their shape and sound into meaning.

So, she did what anyone would do. She googled it.

And it seemed legit; the place had a website with

so much online that it would have been a *lot* of effort just for a scam.

She had gambled on riskier things before.

The writer sees the heru online and wonders if, by the time she is in front of the audience, her hair would be long enough to wear a copy. Wooden, of course; she doesn't have the means to get a heru made of parāoa. Even if she did, she couldn't take it out of the country or bring it overseas.[2] But she's getting ahead—god, she loves a pun—of herself. She's not deciding now, still lying in bed an hour after her alarm. She's not deciding anything until she goes and sees *all* the objects.

But just in case, she'll talk to her hair stylist about growing her layers out.

When she was a teenager, her hair was so long that she could sit on it. She cut it off when she was seventeen, bobbed it just under her jaw. Her father had lamented that loss, convinced that without her "crowning glory" no one would marry her.

Because, of course, discerning gentlemen only care what is on top of your head, not a whit about what's in it.

Gentlemen do not want a woman with wit at all.

And although her jawbone is not as powerful as that of Murirangawhenua, she can still use it as a patu and matau, club and hook, and oh! those words are sharp, and she fights like a mako who has scented blood in the water.

The writer sees the heru in person, behind the well-lit glass of a vitrine and is ...

Underwhelmed.

It is strange to her that a piece that is worn on the head would be so unadorned. But perhaps she has been spoiled by the heru made from beef bone and Dremel and the intricate shapes that the modern carver can make.

Still, the heru she has seen that are similar in appearance and age have at least *some* decoration—the small shape on the side transformed into a manaia, with at least an inlaid paua eye.

This heru seems not only unadorned, but unfinished. A blank waiting to be honed.

Who carved it and where they were from is also blank—its provenance *Zugang ungeklärt*.

It was perhaps abandoned after one of its teeth cracked and broke off. A fault in the bone unseen until carving revealed it.

It is a heru that has never been worn, will never be worn.

She imagines someone digging through a midden to find it, to sell to a collector desperate to acquire pre-contact taonga—and there were slim pickings after the British.

She wonders how the carver would feel that this piece has traveled so far, that centuries after his death his unpolished work is on display. It is a great fear of hers that someone will unearth a rough draft—an idea half-formed—and think it is an exemplar of her work.

Unfinished and unadorned as it is, she can carve her story on it.

She imagines the weight of it in her hand and thinks of the object it once was and the story it will become.

This is where she can get stuck. Turning and turning the possibilities in her mind—because now it could be anything. She could write everything she wants to say about it, of shape and bone and ocean and object.

She splits her work into nine—a part for each tooth, and a part for each space between them. The lie is that each part is discrete, but of course they are connected, they are shape and shadow. They are relief and intaglio.

Mako—sharks in general, but the mako in particular, are known for being aggressive and reckless.
Paua—the shell of the black abalone (*Haliotis iris, Haliotis australis*).

rima

Five a.m. and jetlag is not the only reason I am awake.

Years ago, when I used to work in a government department, I would wake before dawn every morning—even if I was bone-tired—to write. It was the only time I had to devote to my writing, a couple of hours snatched before I had to get ready for work.

Last year, while having drinks with some writers, one of them told me that 3.30 a.m. is the time I should be worried about. According to her, that's when Death is most likely to visit. My 5 a.m. specter is akin to Death, I suppose—at least Death's opening act.

My doctor told me to take walks to help reduce my stress. My blood pressure is far too high and being fat doesn't help, nor does the caffeine I drink. She said I should try to reduce the stress in my life. But I think I'm addicted to it—the thing that stresses me the most lately is the thing that makes me feel the most authentic. How can I cut *me* from my life?

I'm lucky to live so close to the sea. From my house, if I turn left, I can walk to the Southern Coast, and if I turn right, I can walk along the bays into the city. Today I will head to the right, planning to stop at one of the little pebbly beaches along the coast and fill my pockets with sea glass for my collection. Perhaps I'll walk just past Balaena Bay, round the curve of it to see the view of the city. It always delights me—that sudden shift from the wild of the bays to the geometry of the city that hugs the harbor.

I don't know the shape of it, the story I'm supposed to write. I have too many ideas, but nothing to anchor them to yet. Since I moved here, close to the sea, I've always taken walks to rough out my thoughts. Once I settle on an object, a story will come. I worry that there are so many ideas, so many things that I want to say that I cannot say anything at all. I just need the space in my head to hear it speak.

I round the bay, and the headwind is so strong that I have to fight against it every step. And I think of nothing except pushing myself forward. Take another step.

And another.

And another.

Rima—five.

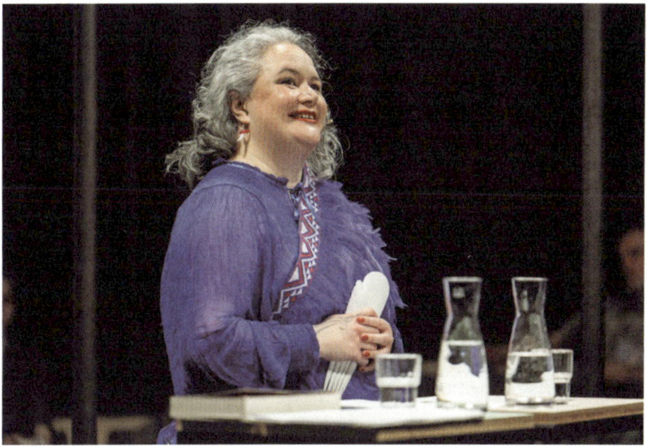

Whiti Hereaka at the Humboldt Forum

Notes

1 With thanks to Irene Albers and Stefan Schawe of Freie Universität Berlin who alerted me to their research on *Tōtō Waka*, appropriated by Romanian avant-gardist Tristan Tzara as his own sound poem in 1920. | **2** CITES (the Convention on International Trade in Endangered Species of Wild Fauna and Flora) prevents the importation of objects made from endangered animals into the signatory countries. The use of whale bone gathered after the whale has died of natural causes is not an exception. In June 2024, the work of Māori artists made from materials gathered from a beached blue whale was denied entry into Hawai'i. The artists were part of a festival of Pacific nations to celebrate the traditional arts of the Indigenous peoples of those nations.

OBJECTS TALK BACK

Priya Basil
Locked In and Out
Preface by Hartmut Dorgerloh

Few buildings are as controversial as the new Berlin Palace, which now houses the Humboldt Forum. In Germany and beyond, people wonder why an imperial palace was rebuilt in the centre of Berlin and then filled with the often violently acquired ethnological collections of the Prussian Cultural Heritage Foundation. The writer Priya Basil unfurls the story of the palace reconstruction alongside a personal story of her migrating to Berlin. She questions what such a building means for our understanding of the past and our sense of belonging in the present. "In German the word Schloss means a palace, and also a 'lock.' The central question: Can a lock also be a key?"

Meena Kandasamy
A Wise One, a Warrior
Preface by Priya Basil

The Mithuna couple is a 17th-century ivory sculpture from Tamil Nadu (India) depicting lovers. Meena Kandasamy examines how caste and class are carved into the object as indelibly as its physical details. She unfurls worlds of possibility around this seemingly idyllic couple, connecting them to personal and political stories that expose painful realities of who gets to love whom. With astonishing narrative flair—mixing X threads, academic discourse, poetry, memoir—she lets the object talk and talk back.

OBJECTS
TALK BACK

Léonora Miano
Ladies of the Throne

Preface by Priya Basil

"Most of the time, it is the power of men that we remember." These words open Léonora Miano's narrative about Mandu Yenu, a throne from the ancient Kingdom of Bamum (present-day Cameroon). The Germans long claimed the object was a "gift" from King Njoya to Kaiser Wilhelm II. Miano reads "between the lines of beads and cowrie shells" to show the complexity of colonial and gender relations. She reveals that Mandu and Yenu were royal wives in the Kingdom of Bamum. The very name of the object suggests it—it is the power of women that we should remember.

Madeleine Thien
The Artisans

Preface by Priya Basil

Canadian writer Madeleine Thien reflects on a fragment of a mural depicting three Uyghur princes from one of the Bezeklik Caves along the Northern Silk Road, in what is now the Xinjiang Uyghur Autonomous Region of China. This most renowned donor portrait of Uyghur-Buddhist art was brought to the Berlin museums following the Second German Turfan Expedition (1904–1905). Thien responds to its vibrant colors and expressive lines with a fictional text, transporting us into the daily lives of the painters who adorned the caves with strikingly lifelike murals in the tenth century. She asks: Is there an autonomous republic of art that transcends time and place?

Published by Stiftung Humboldt Forum im Berliner Schloss

Concept: Priya Basil
Project management: Katharina Kepplinger
Text editing: James Copeland
Image editing: Barbara Martinkat

Special thanks to Fränze Czaja, Han Song Hiltmann and Jan Linders (SHF) as well as to Dorothea Deterts (SMB) for their friendly support.

Federal Government Commissioner for Culture and the Media

Funded by the Federal Government Commissioner for Culture and the Media in line with a resolution by the German Federal Parliament

 The Deutsche Nationalbibliothek lists this publication in the Deutsche Nationalbibliografie; detailed bibliographic data are available on the Internet at http://dnb.dnb.de.

ISBN 978-3-0358-0865-0
Layout: 2edit, Zurich
Printed in Germany

DIAPHANES – Schöneggstrasse 5 – CH-8004 Zurich
DIAPHANES Berlin – Dresdener Strasse 118 – 10999 Berlin – kontakt@diaphanes.net